The Stillness That Embraces the Heart

In the calm of the night, where the silliness flows,
Sleepy faces abound, where the laughter still grows.
Socks might be missing, the cat takes a nap,
Chasing its tail in a whimsical lap.

Under the blankets, the giggles reside,
As pillows support all the dreams we hide.
Imagined adventures with shoes on the wrong,
Dancing with shadows to a silly song.

The clock starts to tick like a jester on cue,
Tickling our senses with a grin, oh so new.
As dreams spin around like the moon on a swing,
We wake up tomorrow and do it again, zing!

In this peaceful embrace, where nonsense can thrive,
With chuckles and smiles, we feel so alive.
Each moment so bright, we float through the night,
In the calm of our dreams, everything feels right.

Original title:
Waves of Tranquil Dreams

Copyright © 2025 Creative Arts Management OÜ
All rights reserved.

Author: Aidan Marlowe
ISBN HARDBACK: 978-1-80587-434-8
ISBN PAPERBACK: 978-1-80587-904-6

Echoes of Serenity Under Stars

Under the sky, a blanket so wide,
Giggling clouds on a lunar slide,
Stars are winking, a cosmic tease,
Fish in pajamas, swimming with ease.

Bubbles of laughter, floating on air,
Dreams in the distance, without a care,
Inner thoughts waltz like a clumsy seal,
While comets humorously spin the wheel.

Floating on a Sea of Reflection

Drifting on puddles of giggling light,
Mirrors of laughter twinkling in flight,
Seagulls are gossiping, squawking with flair,
While dolphins juggle snacks in mid-air.

Sailing on slices of whimsical pie,
Turtles wear hats and give fashion a try,
Reflections chuckle, waves join the spree,
As jellyfish dance like they're wild and free.

The Quiet Dance of Water and Sand

Sandcastles giggle as tides tiptoe by,
Seashells whisper secrets and then slyly cry,
Pebbles are peeking, aligning in rows,
While crabs do a cha-cha, striking a pose.

Ripples that chuckle, ticking like clocks,
Fish in tuxedos tossing tiny rocks,
A conch shell's crooning with nonchalant sass,
As the whole beach joins in, shimmying fast.

Soft Currents of Sleepy Desires

Pillows of silence make cozy beds,
Dreams dressed in clown suits, balancing heads,
Snoozing cats pounce on fluffy old schemes,
As moonlight spills magic on whimsical dreams.

Gentle napping with tickles of night,
A teddy bear juggles, all fluffy and bright,
Whispers of slumber are giggling loud,
As sheep in pajamas prance proud and unbowed.

Holding the Moon in an Open Palm

I caught the moon in my hand,
It slipped right through like soft sand.
I laughed so hard, I missed my chance,
The stars looked down, they shared a glance.

I told the sun, "You're quite a tease,"
With all your rays, you aim to please.
But when I blink, you're gone too soon,
You juggle clouds on a silver spoon.

I chased a comet, running fast,
But tripped and tumbled, what a blast!
It winked at me on its way by,
"You'll need some sparkles if you fly!"

Now night falls gently with a smile,
As I rest my feet for a while.
With laughter in my sleepy dreams,
I'll cradle jokes under moonbeams.

Tidal Dreams Under a Silken Sky

The ocean grinned with bubbles bright,
As fish danced under dim twilight.
I threw a party on the shore,
With jellybeans and laughter galore.

Seagulls squawk, they steal my fries,
While crabs conspire to share their lies.
They boast of treasure, shiny and grand,
But all they have is a broken band.

I surf on dreams, a silly ride,
Till I find my towel's stuck with tide.
I roll and tumble, what a sight!
The seashells laugh - I'm quite the fright!

The sky's a quilt of colors bold,
As midnight tales start to unfold.
I'll dance with starlight, oh so spry,
Under this soft and giggly sky.

Suspended in a Sea of Stars

I hung my hat on a shooting star,
And waved at planets – they're never far.
The Milky Way called out to me,
"Why don't you join this cosmic spree?"

The aliens served me peachy pie,
With laughter spilling as they sigh.
They danced in patterns, quite absurd,
While I just giggled, lost for words.

I rode a meteor, round and round,
Until I landed on marshmallow ground.
"You've got to taste this fluffy spree!"
Cried stars who twinkled joyfully.

Now I float in this silly night,
With cosmic cheer and pure delight.
In the company of sparkly fares,
Forever wed to blissful airs.

The Calm Prelude to a Brighter Dawn

As morning tiptoes through the trees,
I catch a giggle in the breeze.
The flowers sprout with shoes so bright,
And dance with squirrels at dawn's first light.

I brew a potion, silly and warm,
With giggles and whimsy as the norm.
While butterflies chuckle and swoon,
Over muffins baked with a touch of moon.

Chirping birds join the jovial fun,
With tunes that shimmer like the sun.
The grass tickles toes, oh what a tease,
As I try to dance but just sneeze!

And as the day unfurls its sigh,
I watch the clouds roll soft and shy.
With coffee cups and laughter's sway,
A gleeful start to the sunny day.

Murmurs of a Dreaming Shore

Sandy toes with shells to find,
A crab in a tux, quite refined.
Giggles rise with each small splash,
Jellyfish waltz in a jelly stash.

Drifting clouds like fluffy pie,
Seagulls squawk, oh my, oh my!
Sandcastles lean like tired folks,
As surfboards play with quirky jokes.

Celestial Visions on a Liquid Canvas

Stars drop down for a dip and dive,
A fish in a bowtie, oh, it's alive!
Moonbeams giggle, throwing light,
While octopuses dance in moonlight.

Puppies paddle with floppy ears,
Chasing bubbles, eliciting cheers.
Tea parties held on floating logs,
With crumpets served to wise, old frogs.

Harmonies of Dusk and Dawn

Crickets croon as day waves bye,
Fireflies twinkle, blink in the sky.
Cats debate if mice should run,
While raccoons plot their midnight fun.

Sunrise hues like candy smiles,
Fluffy pancakes shared in piles.
With giggles bursting like soft balloons,
Morning welcomes zany tunes.

The Stillness of Misty Horizons

Fog rolls in like a shy guest,
Horses playing dress-up, looking their best.
Llamas grin with hats on their heads,
While hidden fairies whisper in threads.

The world turns slow, a spinning top,
Sipping warm cocoa, let the laughter flop.
Nutty squirrels in a circus act,
Balance acorns, fancy and packed.

Whispered Wishes Beneath the Fading Sun

Beneath the glow of orange skies,
Fish wear hats, to everyone's surprise.
Seagulls debate on sandy trends,
While crabs breakdance, making amends.

A turtle with a secret song,
Sings to seashells that hum along.
Laughter echoes in pelican's flaps,
As dolphins donate to the local mishaps.

The Evening's Blanket Over Silent Waters

A blanket of dusk, with jokes to lend,
Jellyfish giggle as sea cucumbers bend.
Octopuses tease with eight-armed flair,
While starfish plot to give crabs a scare.

The moon winks down, playing coy,
With glowing remarks, like a giggling boy.
Fish play tag through the fading light,
As laughter fills the ocean's night.

Thoughts Adrift in the Gentle Current

In currents that swirl, dreams do flow,
Candy wrappers dance with a whimsical glow.
Electric eels spark up some cheer,
As turtles debate the best pizza here.

Bubbles rise up with silly puns,
Fish wear spectacles and discuss their runs.
A clam blushes deep, what a sight,
As laughter bubbles in the shimmering night.

Canvas of Stars Over a Lullaby Sea

Stars like sprinkles on even tide,
A whale tunes up for a concert ride.
Squid juggle pearls with a wink and cheer,
While shrimp run a marathon, drawing near.

The sky's a canvas, painted with glee,
As seahorses tango, wild and free.
Their laughter mingles with the ocean's hum,
In a fairy tale realm where everyone's dumb.

A Journey Across the Silent Depths

Float along on puffy clouds,
Where fish wear hats and giggle loud.
Bubbles pop in a wild ballet,
Sea turtles dance, come join the fray.

Octopus tales of wriggly cheer,
Sipping tea while casting cheer.
Watch out for the jellybean squid,
Who joins the fun with a crazy skid.

The Embrace of Tides and Timelessness

Seagulls wear sunglasses, oh what a sight,
As crabs play chess with delight at night.
The sand whispers jokes, a sandy sage,
As fish in bow ties take center stage.

Mermaids giggle, their hair in knots,
Trading seashells for silly thoughts.
The ocean laughs, ticklish and bright,
In this watery world, all feels just right.

Ethereal Slumbers in the Salty Air

Dreamy waves sing a lullaby,
While dolphins wear neckties, oh me, oh my!
Starfish conduct the nighttime band,
As the crabs tap dance upon the sand.

Seashells gossip, plot and scheme,
Under the moon, they share a dream.
A starry night where silliness reigns,
In a world where laughter never wanes.

Light and Shadow on the Silent Ocean

Bubbles wiggle in the soft moonlight,
As fish throw parties, what a delight!
Shells make music, a jazzy cheer,
While squids juggle glow sticks, oh my dear!

Crabs in tuxedos dance with flair,
While starfish contemplate life with care.
The tide tickles feet as they prance by,
In this happy place, we'll never cry.

Dusty Shores and Whispered Secrets

On sandy beaches, fair and bright,
The crabs hold meetings, quite a sight.
They gossip softly, in their dance,
About the seagulls, who stole their chance.

With sunburned noses, sunbathers lay,
While sandcastles face the tide's ballet.
A child yells loudly, "Look at me!"
But seagulls laugh, "Just let it be!"

Awakening to a Horizon of Peace

The dawn peeks in with a sleepy grin,
As snoozing fish dream of winning fin.
Turtles stretch in a lazy charm,
While starfish giggle, 'We mean no harm!'

Coffee cups splash, on shores they land,
With sips and slurps, it's truly grand.
Seashells whisper secrets in the sun,
While crabs hold hands, saying, "Just for fun!"

Encounters with the Gentle Tide

The ocean waves played peek-a-boo,
With flip-flops lost, but spirits flew.
Frogs in sunglasses croaked away,
While jellyfish joined the beach ballet.

Seagull slipped, took a nosedive dip,
As kids on shore just laugh and sip.
A beachball rolls, like an unruly pet,
And all join in—'Let's not fret!'

In the Stillness of Ocean Mists

In morning fog, a pirate snores,
While the ocean waves sneak through open doors.
Salty air tickles noses awake,
As crabs tell tales by a big blue lake.

The sun peeks shyly, blushing bright,
And dolphins dance, such a funny sight.
A starfish spills soda for a treat,
And all the shells cheer, running on their feet!

The Celestial Flow of Slumber

In the land where pillows float,
And sheep wear tiny coats,
A cat plays chess with stars,
While dreams slip through the forts.

Blankets dance a jig, oh so bright,
As snoring crabs assist the night,
A bowl of marshmallows rains,
And sleep's the funniest delight.

The moon hiccups a silvery tune,
While a raccoon swings a broom,
Pajamas sprout little feet,
In this whimsical slumber room.

At dawn, the snores collide with light,
A tickle fight, a sleepy sight,
As sunshine paints the sleepy dwell,
In laughter's light, all's very well.

Echoes of the Silent Shore

At the beach where crabs wear hats,
And seagulls dance on stilts,
The ocean whispers goofy rhymes,
To shells that laugh and tilt.

A clam bursts forth a joke or two,
While fish in suits play chess,
The tides tickle the sandy toes,
In postures of soft finesse.

With flip-flops singing silly tunes,
And gulls that dream of flight,
Each wave brings a chuckle near,
In the bright, beaming light.

So if you stroll the sandy lanes,
And hear those giggles roar,
Know that laughter's a treasure here,
On this fun-filled shore.

Ocean's Embrace at Twilight

As dusk drapes the shore in blues,
And sea turtles wear old shoes,
A dolphin serenades the moon,
In a jazzy, wiggly muse.

Octopuses juggle fish with flair,
While crabs do salsa, unaware,
The waves become a dancing stage,
Where dreams slip under, without care.

As stars pop open like confetti,
And jellyfish in skirts look petty,
The twilight hums a zany tune,
While the sea giggles, nice and sweaty.

Embrace the glow, let laughter swell,
As twilight casts its dreamy spell,
In this quirky ocean's night,
Sleep tight, all's goofy and well.

Gentle Riptides of the Soul

In the depths of sleepy thought,
Where even fish have dreams they've caught,
A buoyancy of chuckles reigns,
Where silliness can't be fought.

With a crab that tells a tale so bold,
And starfish wrapped in jokes of old,
The gentlest pull leads to grins,
In currents of laughter, bold as gold.

Like jellybeans that float and sway,
In the currents where giggles play,
The tides tickle the heart's own beat,
In silly rhythms, night and day.

So let your spirit drift along,
In sleepy bliss where laughs belong,
For in the riptides of pure joy,
Every soul sings a funny song.

Fragments of Infinity in a Gentle Breeze

Clouds dance like kittens on fluffy beds,
Chasing each other, bumping their heads.
The sun plays tag with the moon on high,
While seagulls gossip and laugh as they fly.

A sandcastle laughs, it's a sight to see,
With a door that squeaks, and windows of three.
The tide comes in, but it's just a prank,
As crabs wear hats and pretend to be bank.

Jellyfish bounce like balloons on a spree,
Making jokes that only they can foresee.
Stars wink down like they're sharing a joke,
Even the dolphins are smirking, bespoke.

Each blip and splash is a tickle of fun,
In the silly moments beneath the bright sun.
In this playful realm where giggles collide,
Dreams drift like feathers, in laughter we ride.

Glimpses of a Radiant Tranquility

Bubbles float by with a mischievous grin,
Silly little fish wear a curious fin.
The sunset ponders, 'Shall I wear pink today?'
While shells conspire in their secret ballet.

A beach ball rolls like a wayward friend,
Telling tales of sandcastles, bright at the end.
Each grain of sugar, a story to tell,
As crabs give applause, they can't help but yell.

Waves play hopscotch on the golden shore,
Jumping and skipping, forever encore.
The tide whispers secrets to well-tied knots,
While starfish warm up, lending their spots.

Laughter erupts where the ocean meets land,
In the kingdom of mirth, so perfectly planned.
Here, the seagulls wear sunglasses at night,
Promising dreams full of comical light.

The Enchantment of Distant Shores

Fish in tuxedos do a sly little dance,
Seriously funny, they won't leave to chance.
With bubbles that tickle, they giggle and sway,
Enticing the tide to join in their play.

Sand dunes wear hats like a charming parade,
Twisting with breezes, a sight to invade.
A pelican hides, playing peek-a-boo games,
While seaweed dresses up with fanciful names.

Puppy dogs chase crabs, barking with cheer,
As seagulls serve snacks to their friends who are near.
The whole ocean laughs, it's a grand little show,
With shells holding court as the tide flows below.

Under the starlight, the mischief does grow,
As dreams are embroidered with giggles and glow.
Tonight, even the fish wear their best silly hats,
Sharing secrets of whiffs, giggles, and chats.

Twilight's Embrace in Ocean's Hold

As twilight whispers, a giggle takes flight,
Moonbeams are tickled, twisting left and right.
Crabs sprinkle stardust, giggling like kids,
While the ocean wears pjs, hiding its lids.

Lighthouses chuckle, guiding boats with a sway,
They dance in delight to the evening's ballet.
Dandelions tumble, are giddy with grace,
Carrying whispers from their sandy base.

Synchronised swimmers, dolphins parade,
Twisting and flipping in the cool evening shade.
Stars pop like popcorn, and sparkle aloud,
In the laughter of currents, they're proudly endowed.

In the conch-shell's echo, a jester's delight,
Tickling the night with their comical sight.
As dreams take a dip in the cool ocean's fold,
They laugh underwater, where stories are gold.

Secrets Carried by the Breeze

A feather danced down the street,
Chasing pigeons on tiny feet.
Whispers giggle in the air,
As hats fly off with a jaunty flair.

Laughter tickles the sunlit trees,
While squirrels plot in secret ease.
A dog chases a runaway shoe,
In a race known by just a few.

Sugar clouds float on the breeze,
Drawing dreams of sticky cheese.
Where jellybeans grow on vines,
And chocolate spills from moonlit pines.

Each gust brings stories anew,
Of flying trips for a flamboyant crew.
With jellyfish in a funny disguise,
Floating high on laughter's rise.

Shimmering Dreams on the Coast

A crab wears a hat too large to swim,
While seagulls laugh, their faces grim.
Starfish dance in a twinkling row,
Declaring fashion trends we don't know.

Bubbles bounce on sandy shores,
While children yell, 'You're out of scores!'
The ocean smiles with a cheeky grin,
As sandcastles mold where tides begin.

Mermaids sip on coconut milk,
Debating if seaweed's smooth as silk.
A dolphin juggles shells with glee,
As the breeze hums a tune - so carefree.

Crab races spark under the sun,
Who knew shells could be this much fun?
The sea beams bright, a playful tease,
Speculating if fish wear pants like these.

The Stillness Beneath the Surface

In the depths, the fish swim slow,
Playing tag with seaweed's flow.
A grumpy clam gripes about the crowd,
While starfish simply chuckle loud.

Octopuses break out in a dance,
Giving fish a second chance.
A treasure chest hums songs off-key,
With pearls that giggle humorously.

Sand dollars take a sunlit stroll,
Critiquing shells like they're on a roll.
They whisper tales of ancient trips,
While snails compare their slow-motion flips.

Bubble-blowing fish with flair,
Create a symphony in salty air.
There's calmness wrapped in fins and glee,
As laughter bubbles beneath the sea.

Melodies of a Calm Voyage

A ship sails by with a wobbly sound,
While a cat scans the horizon, profound.
The captain snickers, his compass spins,
With jelly on toast always wins.

Lighthouses wave, their beams a dance,
As dolphins perform their graceful prance.
A whale hums tunes that tease the stars,
While sea turtles share their gummy bars.

The anchor sneezes with great delight,
While seagulls squawk about the plight.
Of being stuck in a raucous groove,
Only to find they can't help but move.

Mariners laugh at the clouds up high,
Whispers of storms, a playful lie.
With treasures hidden in pockets deep,
They sail on sound, and sleep on peep.

Nightfall's Silent Serenade

The cat plays piano, oh what a show,
With paws a-tapping, it steals the glow.
Moonlight dances on the sleepy floor,
As snoring dogs dream of chasing a boar.

The stars wink down, like eyes in a plot,
A squirrel in slippers, all snug and hot.
Frogs croak in chorus, a silly old song,
While dreaming goldfish swim with the throng.

Pillow fights rage, in a midnight spree,
As gnomes play charades, so silly, you'll see.
La Lana the llama performs a ballet,
In the land of odd dreams, we all want to stay.

And just when you think this jest couldn't end,
A porcupine giggles, it's quite the trend.
So close your own eyes, let the laughter sprout,
In Nightfall's embrace, joy's what it's about.

Spirit Winds of Infinite Rest

A parrot on holiday, sipping sweet tea,
Wears shades on a branch, just as cool as can be.
Clouds roll by, dressed in cotton delight,
As dreams drift on kites in the dusky light.

The fish all conspire to throw a grand ball,
In the depths of the sea, where seaweed will sprawl.
Octopus limbo, and turtles do waltz,
It's all quite absurd! Who would think of these faults?

Fairy floss wishes float through the sky,
While unicorns giggle, and chickens all fly.
A polar bear dances with clumsy delight,
In a world where the quirky are crowned for the night.

So let every spirit embrace this parade,
For laughter, not fear, is what all dreams made.
Join the odd entities, let jests fly the best,
In the Night's grand delight, find your own jest.

Slumbering Shores of Wonder

An owl is busy, conducting a band,
With beetles and crickets tapping on sand.
The sea whispers secrets, soft as a sigh,
Where mermaids tell tales of a pie in the sky.

Sharks wear tuxedos, all sharp and well-dressed,
While lobsters play chess, they're the true best.
The moon chuckles softly, a giggle so light,
As slumbering fish dream of play fights at night.

A walrus in slippers declares it's a feast,
With cookies and milk, he has quite the least.
So gather your dreams with a grin and a cheer,
For ridiculous wonders will soon disappear.

As dusk's winks abound, don't forget to embrace,
The silliness woven into each space.
Drift off with a smile, let laughter be found,
On Slumbering Shores, where oddness is crowned.

Echoing Dreams Beneath the Sky

In a hammock of clouds, a giraffe snoozes tight,
With stars as his blanket, he's soaring in flight.
The crickets all giggle, the fireflies dance,
At a ball made of magic, they leap at the chance.

A penguin in boots tries to slide down the hill,
But tumbles and rolls with a comical thrill.
While dolphins in tutus perform their grand flip,
Creating a splash that echoes a quip.

The moon's chuckle spreads, like butter on toast,
As shadows of poodles make shapes to boast.
In this land of odd dreams, where laughter is key,
The night fills your heart with wild jubilee.

So let your thoughts flutter, like birds on the breeze,
With nonsense and laughter, you'll forever be pleased.
Join the great antics, beneath endless light,
In Echoing Dreams, let your spirit take flight.

Tidal Hues of Restful Sleep

In slumber's grasp, we snooze away,
Like turtles lost in a buffet tray.
Socks mismatched, we drift and sway,
Dreaming of cakes that save the day.

Feathers tickle, pillows fight,
Snoring beasts disturb the night.
Pajamas on, we take to flight,
In search of snacks, our true delight.

Laughter echoes in our dreams,
With ice cream rivers and fizzy streams.
Banana boats and silly memes,
Life's absurd, or so it seems.

Upon a cloud, we dance and roll,
Karaoke tunes, we lose control.
In this realm where giggles toll,
We find the jokes that feed the soul.

Tranquil Currents of the Heart

Balloons and bubbles parade around,
The cat in a hat, on a scrappy mound.
Dreams of pizza, oh, what a sound,
Heart so light, like a jester crowned.

Wishes float like jellyfish,
Prancing boldly in a sloshy dish.
A donut on a comfy swish,
Holding hands with a quirky fish.

Tickling toes and buttered feet,
Giggling rhymes that can't be beat.
Sunshine giggles in the heat,
As clouds conspire to drop a treat.

With twirls and swirls, we splash and spin,
Belly laughs and a cheeky grin.
In this calm, the fun begins,
We'll dance with dreams, let the party win.

Dances of Echoing Blues

In moonlight's glow, we glide and jive,
With socks that squeak, we come alive.
Chasing fireflies, oh what a dive,
Silly antics make us thrive.

Lost in the rhythm, we trip and spin,
Dodging shadows with a goofy grin.
An orchestra of frogs begins,
As laughter breaks the silent din.

Feeling groovy, we hum a tune,
Under the gaze of a silly moon.
Eat all the snacks, it's never too soon,
Join in the dance, let mischief bloom.

Our hearts beat fast, with joy we sway,
Chasing monotony far away.
In this funky, crazy ballet,
We'll laugh until the break of day.

Embracing the Stillness of the Deep

In quiet moments, we strike a pose,
As fishy friends wiggle their toes.
Bubble gum dreams, in cartoon prose,
With giggles rising, like a rose.

Drifting through sleepy, hunky dory,
Napping pirates with tales of glory.
Each yawning seagull sings a story,
Of treasure maps and pizza tory.

Cuddles with pillows, fears take a leap,
Socks stretched out, not a single peep.
In this calm, our laughter sleeps,
While giddy dreams in silence heap.

We embrace the night with joyous grace,
Welcoming sleep to this funny place.
So close your eyes, join the race,
For sweet nonsense is our saving grace.

Peaceful Horizons in the Night

In a boat made of jelly, I sail on a whim,
The moon gives a wink, my chances are slim.
Fish wear bow ties, they swim with great flair,
While the stars throw a party, their laughter fills air.

The horizon's a canvas, so vast and bright,
With colors of pizza, it's quite a sight.
Seagulls in tuxedos dance on a breeze,
Ordering takeout from tall, leafy trees.

A crab sings a tune, while doing the flail,
And whispers sweet nothings to a passing whale.
The sand tickles toes, they giggle in glee,
As the night stretches on, wild and carefree.

So here's to the night, with all its delight,
Where dreams float like balloons, in joyous flight.
With laughter as soft as the moonlight's gleam,
We drift off to slumber, lost in a dream.

Rippling Reflections of Calm

In a pond full of frogs, who chat and who croak,
I ponder their secrets, is this just a joke?
Lily pads gossip, like teens on a swing,
As the fish play charades, doing their thing.

A turtle in glasses, reading a book,
Looks up, quite annoyed, with one puzzled look.
The sun starts to snooze, throwing gold on the lake,
While ducks plan a prank, for old time's sake.

Reflections of giggles, I see in the tide,
As dragonflies dance, their beauty won't hide.
The breeze carries whispers of silly old tales,
The kind that make sense, like cows in pink sails.

So here's to the ripples, each chuckle and snort,
Let's laugh at the antics, let joy be our sport.
For in these soft moments, so bright and so warm,
We find playful peace, in each silly form.

Murmurs of Starlit Waters

In waters that shimmer, the stars take a dive,
With laughter and splashes, they're trying to thrive.
An octopus yodels, a crab does a jig,
As the moon rolls its eyes, and does a quick dig.

With turtles as judges, we'll have a grand show,
The fish all in costume, they steal the whole glow.
A seaweed conductor waves arms with great zest,
As the bubbles all giggle, they're feeling impressed.

The currents hum softly, like tunes from a horn,
While jellyfish wiggle, bright colors adorn.
The night air is filled with a comical cheer,
As bubbles recite jokes that only fish hear.

So here's to the waters, where silliness flows,
In a splash of mischief, fun magically grows.
With each twinkling star, a secret we keep,
In the heart of the night, where laughter runs deep.

Serenity Sealed in Aqua

A goldfish with glasses debates with a cat,
About who is wiser, and which hat looks fat.
Seashells are giggling, they tumble and roll,
As sea cucumbers ponder their next big goal.

A dolphin does cartwheels, with flair that astounds,
While jellyfish boogie, floating with sounds.
The tide sets a rhythm, it's party time here,
With seaweed confetti and oceans of cheer.

We dance with the clams, under soft, starry skies,
As mermaids trade gossip, with playful wisecries.
The fish form a choir, singing silly old tunes,
While crabs join the chorus, with scoots and with prunes.

A toast to the waters, where giggles are found,
With sloshing and splashes, in laughter unbound.
So let's dive into joy, with hearts light as foam,
In a world full of whimsy, we find our sweet home.

Echoing Reveries from the Abyss

Fish wear glasses, swimming in style,
They gossip and giggle, chat for a while.
With bubbles like giggles, under bright sun,
They plan a grand party, oh, what fun!

A crab brings the snacks, a feast for the crew,
While dolphins juggle shells, laughter anew.
Octopus DJ spins, with eight arms on the beat,
As turtles do the moonwalk, moving their feet.

Jellyfish glow softly, like tiny bright lights,
They dance in the water, under starry nights.
But hold on a minute, what's that on a hook?
A whale in a tutu, oh, what a look!

So down in the depths, where the colors are bold,
The dreams are quite silly, more fun than gold.
With friends all around, every splash is a cheer,
In this quirky abyss, there's nothing to fear!

Reflections on the Glassy Surface

The pond is a mirror, so shiny and bright,
Where frogs wear crowns, it's quite the sight.
They leap with a flair, discussing grand schemes,
And sing silly songs, tangled up in dreams.

A duck tries ballet, slips into a spin,
While turtles in tuxedos grin, witness the din.
The reeds sway and giggle, whispering jokes,
As fish play charades, in the midst of these folks.

The dragonfly's gossiping, all dressed up in flair,
Complains of her hairdo, blown wild by the air.
The goldfish just chuckles, all cozy in green,
Declaring their pond the best stage ever seen!

With each splash of laughter, the calm never fails,
In a world where the funny swims, life tells tales.
With petals as hats, and the sun in a glee,
These reflections hold secrets, as bright as can be!

Serenading the Shimmering Silhouette

At dusk on the shore, with rhythms of the tide,
A seagull named Sally finds shells to reside.
She struts and she caws, with flair and with pride,
Wearing clams as her jewels, a true seaside guide.

The sun throwing glitter, a sparkling mess,
As crabs join the dance, in their shiny red dress.
They move with a shuffle, one step, then a slide,
While the starfish take selfies, trying to hide.

A hermit crab chimes in, with tales of his home,
"I wish it was bigger, but hey, I can roam!"
With laughter erupting, the ocean's delight,
The silhouettes singing, till blankets of night.

And when the moon beams, with a wink and a sway,
The jokes come in waves, like a playful ballet.
In this shimmering glow, where laughter sets free,
The serenades echo, like waves of glee.

Beneath the Surface of Calm Waters

Under the surface, where the tickles arise,
Fish feasting on bubbles, wearing surprised eyes.
They play peek-a-boo, with a wink and a grin,
In a world filled with giggles, let the fun begin!

The seaweed waves wildly, dancing with might,
As the orange clownfish leads a conga line bright.
With every fin flapping, it's a joyous parade,
As the octopus juggles, a splashing charade!

The dolphins come singing, in harmony's flow,
Turning tides into tunes, putting on quite the show.
With joy in their flips, and the sea as their stage,
Life beneath waters bursts forth with a craze!

So here in the calm, where the deep secrets rest,
Laughter bubbles over, it's really the best.
In this jubilant dance, let worries be free,
As dreams make a splash, like faraway glee!

Whispering Shores of Peace

On sandy beds, we wiggle our toes,
As gulls above speak in silly prose.
With sun hats askew, we wiggle and laugh,
Like crabs in a dance, we're nature's half-calf.

The tide tickles toes, a gentle embrace,
As we sip on drinks, with foam on our face.
A seagull steals chips, oh what a delight,
We chase him away, but he gives us a fright!

Flip-flops are flying, hats taking a flight,
While shadows are laughing in the golden light.
Through giggles we wander, we're lost in the fun,
Like children at play, frolicking under the sun.

As sandcastles crumble, our masterpieces fall,
We cheerfully bury ourselves, laughing at all.
In the whispering breeze, our joys intertwine,
At these shores of laughter, all worries decline.

Beneath the Veil of Aquamarine

Under the shimmer of a turquoise sheet,
We paddle our feet, what a comical feat!
Mermaids might giggle, if they only could see,
As we splash like fish, wildly giddy and free.

A dolphin appeared, gave us quite the shock,
He flashed a great grin, was that part of his schtick?
We tried to impress with our synchronized dance,
But only did flounders grant us a glance!

With rubbery ducks bobbing close by,
We float and we chatter as seagulls high fly.
Beneath the vast blue, we search for a star,
In search of the laughter that's never too far.

Our picnic's a mix of snacks, a nice spread,
With crumbs in our laps, and crumbs on our head!
So here's to our laughter, the joy that it brings,
Beneath the bright canopy, we'll dance like spring things.

Ocean's Whispering Serenade

The ocean hums softly, a tune out of tune,
With crabs as the chorus, they croon to the moon.
Flip-flops are squeaking, our laughter's the beat,
As jellyfish jiggle, quite fancy, quite neat.

We build quirky towers with shovels in hand,
While a rogue little wave makes a quick, daring stand.
A sandcastle army, under our command,
Falls victim to giggles, our plans just unplanned!

With each little splash, our worries suspend,
As seaweed adorns us, our own fashion trend.
We're pirates of laughter, with treasure to find,
In the melodies echoing, our souls are aligned.

So here in the surf, where the silly reside,
We dance with the tide, our laughter our guide.
As the sun slowly sinks, our joy does not tire,
In the ocean's embrace, our spirits aspire!

Lullabies of the Midnight Tide

The moon's a big cookie, the stars all agree,
While waves play a song, as sweet as can be.
In pajamas and dreams, we're lost in delight,
With giggles and whispers, we conquer the night.

The crickets are DJs, the breeze sways to a beat,
As we count all the fishes with fins and with feet.
We dance in our slippers, round and round we spin,
In the magic of night, let the laughter begin!

A sandman appears, with a top hat and cane,
He offers us stories from the endless domain.
With marshmallows roasting and sharks dressed in tux,
Our midnight adventures leave us all quite perplexed.

So here we will snuggle, as stars start to flee,
On pillows of laughter, we drift out to sea.
With lullabies swaying, our dreams take to flight,
As the moon keeps on chuckling, goodnight, sleep tight!

Silhouttes of Daydreams at Twilight

In twilight's glow, the shadows sway,
Where giggling clouds play hide and seek.
A cat in a hat recites ballet,
While stars in pajamas do peek.

Mice in tuxedos dance on the sand,
Holding tiny umbrellas, oh so bright.
A turtle takes a jazz band stand,
Jiving under the moon's soft light.

With dreams of marshmallows in the breeze,
Silly thoughts ride the sparkling waves.
Laughter tumbles like leaves from trees,
In a world where imagination behaves.

The cosmic party, a grand soirée,
Hosts rubber ducks in a moonlit flow.
Chasing each other, all in dismay,
As the night shows off a radiant glow.

Threads of Peace Woven on the Shore

Seagulls chase crabs in a merry round,
As driftwood tells tales from the past.
Breezes gossip, oh what a sound,
With jellyfish shimmering, vast.

Sandcastles play dress-up in pride,
Sporting seashell hats and jelly shoes.
Turtles play tag with the gentle tide,
While pufferfish share their daily blues.

Laughter dances with the salty mist,
As flip-flops mambo on textured sand.
A clam forgot its bucket list,
And dreams of flying to neverland.

Mermaids giggle, tangled in nets,
Trading seashells for poofy hair.
The ocean's secrets, full of regrets,
Cheerful moments floating in air.

The Echo of Whispers in the Night

Under the stars, the crickets croon,
While owls wear glasses, reading the sky.
The moon plays piano, oh such a tune,
As fireflies giggle and twinkle nearby.

A snail in a top hat takes his sweet time,
Contemplating life, or maybe a dance.
Bubbles float past like a whimsical rhyme,
As dreams create a frolicsome trance.

Bats hold a meeting in the old oak tree,
Discussing snacks and the best flying route.
While raccoons debate who's the cutest, you see,
And all of their chit-chat is rather astute.

With whispers soft as a pillow's embrace,
The night wears laughter like a warm coat.
In dreams' hidden corners, such a lively place,
Where humor floats freely, sailing a boat.

Allure of the Unseen Horizon

Beyond the mountains, a secret spills,
Where socks go to live, and shoes find glee.
Horizons yawn and share their thrills,
While llamas tell jokes with cups of tea.

Kites made of dreams flap in the breeze,
Waving goodnight to the golden sun.
A turtle in shades says, "Life's a tease!"
While jellybeans frolic, oh, what fun!

As giggles stretch over hills so steep,
A compass spins wildly, lost in toast.
With whispers of secrets, in harmony deep,
They celebrate joy, toasting their boast.

Mysteries laugh in the edge of the sea,
With umbrellas for fish and hats for the whales.
In this old ballet where all is carefree,
Horizon giggles as each moment sails.

Floating Thoughts on a Crystal Sea

On a boat made of marshmallows, I float,
The seagulls yell, "Hey, you forgot your coat!"
Jellyfish giggle in a pancake parade,
While dolphins dance in the lemonade shade.

My worries are bubbles that pop with a squawk,
The fish are all dancing, they're learning to talk.
A crab on a surfboard gives me a cheer,
As waves toss my thoughts to the shore—never fear!

Stars in the sky wear their pajamas with style,
While the moon bakes cookies, it stays for a while.
Clouds serve up cotton candy with glee,
As I sip on my dreams like they're brewed herbal tea.

Laughter and silliness fill up the air,
I'm sailing through giggles, it's wonderfully rare.
On a sea full of chuckles, I drift without shame,
In this marshmallow haven, I play a fun game.

Sunlit Horizons of Quietude

I spotted some mermaids, they're sipping cool tea,
One drooled in surprise—hey, that one looks like me!
The sunflowers wear hats made of seaweed and glee,
While the breeze sings softly, it's quite the spree.

I stumbled on turtles trying to breakdance,
They twisted and turned, oh what a chance!
A sandcastle prince offers me popcorn, quite grand,
While seagulls applaud with their wings in hand.

The clouds juggle rainbows, a colorful sight,
As squirrels in sunglasses play catch with the light.
The horizon is giggling, it's bursting with cheer,
In this silly escape, I feel no fear.

As seashells write poems in the frothy foam,
The horizon whispers, "You are always home."
With laughter as my compass, I sail through the day,
In this sunlit joyride, I surely will stay.

Drift into Gentle Illusions

A fish in a tuxedo sings cabaret tunes,
While octopuses paint with the light of the moons.
The seaweed does pirouettes, oh what a sight,
As turtles play cards under starlight so bright.

Each wave tells a secret in glimmers and laughs,
The sand tickles toes, like ticklish giraffes.
I found a lost shoe and called it my pet,
Together we giggle, it's a pair I won't fret.

There's a parrot in sneakers, he's mime-ing a tale,
With a wink and a squawk, he sets up the sail.
Flying fish laugh as they bounce on the glow,
While I drift in my dreams, as the soft breezes blow.

I ride on a surfboard made out of cheese,
With jellybeans sailing, I'm totally at ease.
In this quirky adventure, I revel and play,
As the sea of my dreams sweeps my worries away.

The Calm Between the Tides

In a hammock of sea foam, I sway without care,
While a clam offers snacks, it's quite the affair.
The sailboats are giggling, they race for a cause,
With anchors made of donuts, oh, what a pause!

I met a wise duck with a hat and a cane,
He quacked of adventures through sunshine and rain.
Seashells play bingo, as crabs cheer for fun,
In the calm, silly breezes, we're never outdone.

The starfish hold court on a throne made of sand,
With jelly beans glistening, it's truly unplanned.
A seagull recites poetry, quite eloquent, you see,
While the sun joins the laughter, it shines joyfully.

As I lounge in this bliss like a king on his throne,
The world keeps on laughing, and I'm never alone.
In the calm of this moment, let silliness flow,
And let each giggle ripple, like waves in the glow.

Floating Ashore on Cotton Clouds

I drift upon a fluffy fluff,
With seagulls wearing hats so tough.
Each breeze a tickle, every sigh,
I laugh as lollipops float by.

A jellybean sun begins to rise,
While clouds engage in silly cries.
Coconuts juggle in the sky,
As I sip lemonade, oh my!

The moon slips in with a grin so wide,
And stars dance like they can't abide.
I join the show, I wiggle free,
On marshmallow shores, just let me be.

The tide rolls in with a goofy wave,
My toes make footprints, oh how they crave!
In this sweet circus, I'll forever dwell,
Floating ashore, I bid fare thee well.

Serenades of Solitude at Dusk

As crickets play their evening tunes,
I wrestle shadows, hum to the moons.
My cat conducts from a chair of grass,
While the fireflies practice their ballet class.

Near a pond where frogs hold court,
They sport tiny hats for their nightly sport.
I join the ruckus, croak a bit loud,
A solo performance for the idling crowd.

The trees sway like they're having a ball,
Whispering secrets that I can't recall.
Laughter bubbles up from the ground,
In this twilight hakuna matata found.

With a nod to the owls, I take my leave,
Swaying softly, I begin to weave.
In solitude, I find such delight,
Under the stars, giggling at night.

Ripples of Memory on the Water's Surface

A rubber duck floats, taking its time,
With sunglasses on, it looks sublime.
It tells tales of a bath gone wild,
Of sudsy adventures and a laughing child.

The old fish winks, he knows the score,
With each ripple, he fondly recalls more.
A crab in a tux tips his shell with flair,
While the water tickles without a care.

I toss a pebble, splashes fly high,
Under a chuckling, popcorn sky.
Memories ripple, in giggles they play,
Floating on bubbles till the end of the day.

The pond whispers softly, "Come back, come see,"
Where laughter is trapped in serene jubilee.
With each gentle wave, a story retold,
In a splash of joy, the heart turns to gold.

Corners of the World Bathed in Light

In the corners where the sunshine beams,
Silly penguins dance in cartoonish dreams.
With sun hats perched at a jaunty angle,
They laugh and play, joyfully wrangle.

There's a squirrel with a stash of nuts,
Who juggles acorns while laughing a lot.
With each drop, he giggles at fate,
"Can't catch me now, I'm running late!"

Butterflies wear socks, what a sight,
Flapping about, oh what pure delight!
While daisies gossip in whispers so sweet,
About the grasshopper's tap dancing feet.

The sun waves hello, and so does the moon,
Each corner alive with joy that's in tune.
In this jolly realm, let merriment thrive,
As laughter and light keep our spirits alive.

Nightfall's Embrace on the Bay

As the sun dips low in the sky,
The fish start to giggle and fly.
Crabs in tuxedos tap dance,
While seagulls join in for a chance.

The moon takes a seat on a chair,
Waves whisper tales of the fair.
Stars yawn and flicker their lights,
The night's a stage, oh what sights!

Bubbles bounce in a silly show,
While jellyfish glide to and fro.
Laughter echoes off the shore,
Cracking up, we all want more!

And as the tide pulls back its hand,
Each wave has a life that's quite grand.
With rubber duckies brave and bold,
Their tales of laughter will be told.

Dreamscapes in an Ocean of Stars

In a world where dreams go swimming,
Starfish do karaoke, all grinning.
A moonbeam plays on a fiddle,
While comets dance, oh what a riddle!

Mermaids trade gossip and jokes,
As narwhals juggle with strokes.
The milky way sways like a tune,
While dolphins make plans for balloons.

Turtles in top hats spin around,
While dreaming of cupcakes, they're found.
Past the clouds, the stars shout out,
In this realm, there's never a doubt!

A fish in a bowtie serves cake,
With sprinkles of laughter to wake.
As night time giggles fill the air,
The dreams keep rolling without a care.

The Peaceful Melody of Distant Shores

On shores where the sun likes to play,
Sandy toes say, "Hip-hip-hooray!"
Seashells tell tales of the breeze,
As crickets harmonize with ease.

A wave sneezes, it's quite absurd,
Out pops a fish with a word.
The gulls chuckle, riding the tide,
Sharing secrets they cannot hide.

Children chase shadows at dusk,
Tickling crabs—oh, what a fuss!
Every splash is a shimmering laugh,
The shore is a joyous photograph.

So join in the splash and sway,
Let the tides guide you to the play.
For laughter is the song of the sea,
A reminder of how fun life can be!

Deep Blue Reflections of the Soul

In the depths of the ocean so wide,
Fish wear glasses, what a sight!
Giggling echoes in each shiny scale,
As octopuses tell funny tales.

A wise old turtle spins like a top,
Saying, "Don't forget, it's okay to flop!"
Sea cucumbers laugh with delight,
At being so squishy and light.

Stars in the water twinkle and tease,
A dolphin winks, "Life's a breeze!"
With every bubble that floats up high,
Dreams are just laughter that fly.

So delve into depths, take a dip,
Feel the giggles on your trip.
For the soul is bright when it's free,
Swimming along, oh joy, oh glee!

Dreaming in the Cradle of the Sea

In a boat made of jelly, I float with delight,
My fishy friends giggle, what a curious sight.
They tickle my toes as they dance all around,
Bubbles and laughter, the best joys I've found.

A crab plays the violin, a seagull sings high,
While the seaweed waltzes, under the sky.
With each splash and each giggle, the stars start to twirl,
In this silly adventure, oh how the waves swirl!

The octopus juggles with shells and with glee,
Silly smiles swim by, bringing joy to the sea.
A dolphin in sunglasses does flips for a cheer,
In this ocean of nonsense, happiness is near.

As the tide carries dreams on its frothy crest,
We giggle and float, in our sea-hugging nest.
With each wave of laughter, together we beam,
In the cradle of silliness, we're living the dream.

The Suspension of Time Above Water

Floating on a noodle, I drift through the day,
Time takes a vacation, it's gone far away.
The clock on the sand says it's time for a snack,
But I'll just keep swimming, there's no looking back.

A turtle named Gary has stolen my fries,
He wears a top hat and a pair of spies.
We barter for cookies, a fair fishy deal,
This underwater party, it's all surreal!

The sun takes a break, while the stars have their fun,
We're counting all jellyfish, one by one.
With laughter like bubbles, we light up the night,
The world turns to giggles, in pure delight.

So let's float on a dream, on our wobbly throne,
As the tides carry tales of a realm all our own.
In this realm of the funny, where moments align,
Time means nothing here, oh isn't it fine?

Radiant Thoughts Beneath Soft Skies

Under skies painted laughter, we jig in the sun,
With dreams made of giggles, our fun's just begun.
Clouds wearing pajamas drift lazily by,
While rainbows do cartwheels, oh my, oh my!

Cotton candy mountains and rivers of cake,
Here in our silly world, there's no chance to wake.
With spoonfuls of sunshine, we sprinkle some glee,
In this land of the fanciful, we'll always be free.

We chase after shadows, with bubbles and cheer,
A squirrel named Larry likes to whistle while near.
Each giggle that echoes, like notes on a breeze,
In this radiant playground, we do what we please.

So let's dance with the daisies, and sing with the trees,
In this whimsical moment, we live with such ease.
With radiant thoughts swirling like leaves in the air,
Every heartbeat's a joke, oh how lighthearted we fare!

Illuminations from the Depths of Tranquility

Down in the deep, where the silliness lurks,
An eel in a tuxedo is making some quirks.
He tells jokes to a clam, who replies with a grin,
In this underwater giggle, where fun will begin.

The jellyfish glow like the stars in a line,
Their pulsing light patterns, oh how they divine!
With squishy companions, we bounce up and down,
Creating a symphony, wearing laughter as crown.

An underwater disco with shrimp and with flares,
We dance through the bubbles, with no time for cares.
As sea turtles shuffle and fish shimmy close,
In this realm of the funny, we toast to the most!

So dive in the joy, let the laughter unite,
With echoes of friendship, we'll glide through the night.
In illuminations bright, from the depths we emerge,
With each joyful giggle, all worries we'll purge.

www.ingramcontent.com/pod-product-compliance
Lightning Source LLC
Chambersburg PA
CBHW060146230426
43661CB00003B/589